ST PATRICK

HIS LIFE & LEGEND

by

Hector McDonnell

To my friend Patrick, a saver of plants, rather than souls.

I am deeply indebted to the many scholars past and present who have thought far longer, deeper and harder about Patrick than I, most particularly John Bannerman, Ludwig Bieler, Cormac Bourke, J. Carney, D. A. Binchy, Hubert Butler, R. P. C. Hanson, A. B. E. Hood, D. R. Howlett, Liam de Paor, & E. A. Thompson. Patrick's own words, the *Confession* and *Letter*, have appeared in various editions and translations. I am equally indebted to the superb writings of Elaine Pagels on Gnosticism and early Christianity, which have been of enormous help and inspiration.

Who were you, Patrick?

The names you give pass deftly through our touch,
Your village lives on no one's map;
Were you in Mayo or was it Slemish hill
Did burly men press nipples to your lips?

Somewhere
you cried out to your half-known god
And saw him slide within your body's frame
Talking to soothe and urge you on.

But who was then the emperor?
Who called you vile? Where did you go?
We cannot know, though even now
Your guardians watch within the mountain peaks
and wait.

CONTENTS

Introduction	1
I Patrick	2
Visions	4
Romano-British Beginnings	6
On the World's Edge	8
Escaping Slavery	10
The Irish Mission	12
Bishop Patrick	14
Accusations	16
Light of the World	18
Into the Dark Ages	20
Tírechán and Muirchú's Patrick	22
Slemish and Skerry	24
Easter at Tara	26
The End of Pagan Ireland	28
Armagh	30
Voclut	32
Wonder Tales	34
Croagh Patrick	36
Lughnasa Hills & Waters	38
Away with the Fairies	40
Holy Ancestors	42
Glastonbury	44
Relics	46
Lough Derg	48
Snakes and Shamrocks	50
St Patrick's Day	52
Saint Paddy	54
Sites Associated with St Patrick	56
Chronology	58

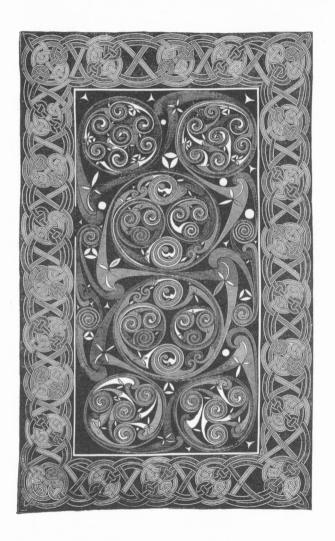

INTRODUCTION

Saint Patrick is a most intriguing figure. His career probably spans the mid fifth century, though we cannot be precise, and there are continuing arguments about whether he was a generation or so later or earlier. He was born into the Romano-British gentry but much of his life was spent in Ireland, where he wrote his two extraordinary works, the Confession and Letter to the Soldiers of Coroticus. These are the only surviving texts from the British Isles during the century which saw the departure of the Roman legions and the rise of the Anglo-Saxons in Britain, and the start of Ireland's transformation from a largely pagan, illiterate, barbarian society into a haven of learning, Christianity and literacy.

Patrick's texts are tantalising. It is extremely hard to identify any of the people or places he mentions, and even if we do they just leave us with more questions which we cannot answer. He wrote in Ireland in Latin, apparently to Romano-British churchmen and leaders back in Britain with whom he was in dispute, though only copies kept in Ireland survived, the sole remnants, apart from a few scraps, of what must once have been a considerable quantity of Romano-British literature.

I have attempted here to give a picture of Patrick's life based on his own words, as well as some indications of its context, and I follow this with the main beliefs and traditions which accumulated round him. These were collected, or arose, many long years later, but there appear to be fragments of real memories of Patrick embedded in them, as well as extraordinary glimpses into Ireland's pagan and early Christian past. I leave it to the reader to look, and think, speculate and question.

I PATRICK
an Irish Roman

EGO PATRICIUS PECCATOR RUSTICISSIMUS Et minimus omnium fidelium. "I, Patrick, a sinner, extremely rural, and the least of all the faithful."

Thus begins Saint Patrick's *Confession*, his response to complaints made in Britain about his work in Ireland. He crams in biblical quotations, and divides it into five parts in imitation of the Pentateuch, lambasting his detractors in erudite if awkward prose. He is God's chosen instrument, working on the world's edge and preparing for the 'final days' by giving the Gospel to this furthest nation in expectation of Christ's imminent return.

Unlike St Augustine's *Confession* of 398, which is a fluid, anecdotal, intellectual quest, Patrick wrote in dense metres inspired by his Latin Bible. He frequently used the chiasmus to create contrasting, mirror-image phrases and also the golden section to place important ideas at 'extreme' and 'mean' ratio positions in the text, while in his *Letter* God's name comes on lines that are multiples of seven, a symbol of the Creation.

His critics have vanished, but Patrick's words remain.

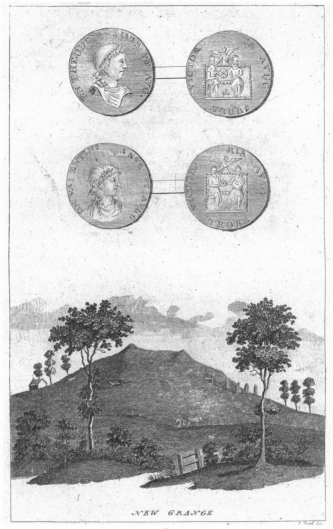

NEW GRANGE

T. Ford Sc.

VISIONS
the voice of god

Patrick says he had seven supernatural experiences, mostly in dreams, and in highly stressed circumstances. The first came when he was a slave, and heard God say a ship would take him home. While trying to get there he wandered starving for three weeks, then feasted on pork and experienced sleep paralysis, a sensation of being confined by a heavy weight and unable to move. Patrick believed this was a satanic attack. The third experience came after he had been, some years later, put in prison. A voice came to him telling him that his captivity would end in two months. In the fourth, while he was living in Britain after escaping from slavery, he heard the Irish calling out for his return.

In the fifth Patrick heard 'holy words I could not yet understand' and a voice saying 'He who gave his own soul for you is He who speaks in you,' while in the sixth he felt that he saw the Holy Spirit 'inside me praying, as if I were inside my own body, and I heard above me, that is above the interior man, how He prayed most strongly in groans.'

Such an intense personal relationship with God did not tie in at all comfortably with the concepts of the Roman state church, which saw itself as the only vehicle of spirituality. Patrick's last vision came after he was criticised, and gives a particularly Gnostic view of closeness to God, who spoke to him saying 'we have seen with disapproval' Patrick's accuser. He commented that God had used 'we' to show how 'he has joined himself to me, just as if he had said that he who touches you touches the pupil of my eye.'

ROMANO-BRITISH BEGINNINGS
amongst the gentry

'My father was Calpornius, a deacon, son of Potitus, a presbyter. I was captured at the village of Bannavem Taberniae, (or Bannaventa Berniae) where he had a little villa.' They were rural landed gentry and local town councillors, decurions, with a villa staffed by slaves, presumably in western Britain. The family was not religious, Patrick tells us, although his father and grandfather were priests. Constantine had exempted Christian clergy from tax obligations, and though aspirant clergy members had to give away their property Patrick's family had used this tax dodge without losing their villula.

Christianity in Western Europe at this time was basically the religion of Roman cities, officialdom, magnates and slaves. The word pagan from *paganus*, rural, well illustrates the social divides. Earlier beliefs, culminating with Neoplatonism, had devised a spiritual hierarchy which mirrored the Roman imperial system and were the model for the Christian heaven; the gods were satellites or emanations of a supreme deity personified as Sol Invictus or Helios, the sun, much like the relationship of Christian angels, saints and devils to the Trinity. Emperor Julian promoted the older heliocentric beliefs again in the 360s but its geocentric Christian counterpart triumphed. Goddess Victory's statue left the senate in 381, and pagan worship was a crime after 395, though the old beliefs hung on.

Revolts and barbarian invasions intensified. Alaric sacked inviolable Rome in 410, and a year later the emperor told the British to fend for themselves, though Britain still thought itself Roman for decades, and Patrick considered Roman citizenship a Christian norm.

Above: Early 6th Century mosaic of the Emperor Justinian and entourage, from San Vitale, Ravenna; Below: 4th century mosaic from Hinton St Mary, Dorset.

ON THE WORLD'S EDGE
a barbarian's slave

When Patrick was sixteen, Irish raiders appeared, 'devastated' the place, murdered many, and took him captive. He became a slave presumably near 'Voclut wood by the Western sea,' the only Irish place he mentions. This seems to be Foghill, near Killala in Mayo, in an area which has the highest density of raths or ring forts in Ireland, evidence of an active and expanding society. The raths are mostly later, but the cultural revitalisation which transformed Ireland had begun by Patrick's time, and the changes included the adoption of sub-Roman tools, crops, dairying and other agricultural methods along with the introduction of individual land tenure instead of a tribal, communal organisation.

'After I came to Ireland I tended the livestock every day, and often prayed. More and more love and fear of God came to me, my faith increased and my spirit was so aroused that I would say a hundred prayers in one day and at night almost the same. On the mountains or before dawn I rose to pray, in snow, in frost, in rain.'

There were over a hundred Irish kingdoms inside Ireland's tribal 'fifths' or provinces, noblemen measured wealth in cattle, and assemblies or fairs were held on sacred hills. They were fascinated by the Romans, wore imitation Roman belts, swords and armour and a few could even write. A native script, ogham, was invented for inscriptions on Irish standing stones, and in their British colonies, emulating Latin monuments, and there were Christians both amongst the Irish and the 'thousands' of British slaves.

Above: A rath, or ring-fort. Right: Irish costume of St Patrick's time. Below: The Tara Brooch. Below right: The secret Ogum alphabet.

1 Ogum Croabh		O Sullivan's Ogum		2 Britifh Ogum		
Charact.	Power	Character	Power	Char.'	Pow.	Name
	B		B		a	Alap
	L		L		b	Braut
	N		F		c	Curi
	T		S		d	Dexu
	H		N		e	Egin
	M		H		f	Feh
	D		D		g	Guidir
	C		T		h	Hurl
	Q		C		i	Jechuit
	Mg		M		k	Kam
	Ng		G		l	Louber
	Sd		ng		m	Mum
	R		R		n	N'hn
	A		A		o	Cr
	O		O		p	Parth
	U		U		q	Quith
	E		E		r	Rat
	I		I		s	Trans
			ia		u	Sung
			ai		x	Vir
			oi		z	Seil
			ua		ae	Qff
			eg		au	Zair
			fto		ei	Auur
			cai			Eftaul
			eai			Egui
						Aur
						Emo
						Kenc
						Blau

9

ESCAPING SLAVERY
visions and pledges

One night, while fasting, presumably as a self-imposed religious discipline, Patrick had his first vision. 'It is good that you fast, as you will soon go home,' a voice said. 'Look! Your ship is ready.'

He escaped across two hundred miles of Irish terrain, and found a departing boat. Its captain initially refused Patrick, though he offered the 'wherewithal' for his travel, but then the crew invited him, even though he refused to suck their nipples. (This must have been a ritual for binding oaths of loyalty and is the only information Patrick gives about pagan customs. Male nipples must have had a particular symbolic significance in Ireland: an Irish Iron Age human sacrifice recently found in a bog had his nipples cut off.) Instead Patrick said he would 'come in the faith of Jesus Christ.'

I suspect the crew intended offering their services in Britain as mercenaries or labourers, and took Patrick along as a useful guide. On arrival they 'wandered through wasteland' for twenty-eight days, starving. Were they keeping low until they found a community that wanted them? The captain taunted Patrick that his Christian god was not helping them, he refused some honey as it came from a pagan offering, but they all 'gave great thanks to God' when they came upon a flock of pigs, which they slaughtered and feasted on. After that, and probably suffering from the effects of a glut of pork on a starved stomach, Patrick had his sleep paralysis experience at dawn the next morning.

THE IRISH MISSION
a message from Voclut

After his escape Patrick became a priest in Britain, but wanted to go back to Ireland. 'A few years later,' he relates, 'I was with my parents again,' who pressed him not to go, as did Church colleagues, but he dreamt of 'a man coming as from Ireland called Victoricius with countless letters ... I heard voices of those near Voclut wood by the western sea who exclaimed with one voice we ask you, holy boy, to come and walk amongst us.'

Victoricius is the only person named in St Patrick's *Confession*. An ecclesiastic with this name, probably Romano-British, was bishop of Rouen and an important follower of St Martin. Like Martin, and in contrast to St Augustine, he followed the old Christian principle of active non-violence. He founded rural monastaries and missions to barbarians north of Gaul. He came to Britain to 'teach the precepts of the martyrs' and worked with its bishops on unspecified issues in 396. If he inspired or organised the mission to Ireland this would explain why Patrick gives his name.

The Irish Christian community was significant enough by 431 for the pope to send his own secretary, Palladius, as their first bishop. He had worked with Germanus of Auxerre to suppress Pelagius' teachings in Britain (St Jerome called the British-trained Pelagius a 'porridge-fed Scotus,' so Irish by origin). The Christian communities in southeast Ireland seem to have had some clergy from Gaul, such as Secundinus, Auxilius and Iserninus, whose hilltop churches were near royal hill sites, while Declán, Ailbe, Ibar and Ciarán were British or Irish. There were also priests from Britain and Gaul working in north Leinster, the midlands, close to Tara and beside Cruachan, the royal hill site of Connacht.

BISHOP PATRICK
spreading the gospel

A British church synod must have later elected Patrick as bishop and Irish mission leader. He says he converted thousands, including slaves and women, and like bishops Martin of Tours (d. 397) and Victiricius of Rouen brought monastic and ecclesiastical organisation to backward rural societies. He says he ordained many priests and monks, women became 'virgins of Christ' (an individual ascetic observance) and reputedly his disciple Mochta, another Briton, founded the first known Irish monastery at Louth.

Patrick states that he took the Gospel to remote areas where no Christians had ever been, and that he returned to Voclut. The only other clear information he gives us is that he worked amongst the Scoti, a north Irish tribal group (it is therefore most intriguing that St Jerome says Pelagius is a 'Scotus'). Patrick says the Scoti had 'worshipped only idols and unclean things, but now a people of the Lord has been made, and are called sons of God. Sons and daughters of Scoti chieftains are openly monks and virgins of Christ.' Even a young Scota woman of very high birth, he says, had become a Christian virgin.

He was imprisoned, threatened with death and put in fetters, but also held high status, for he gave gifts to kings and 'judges,' brehons. Great men did not take gifts from inferiors, so this was significant, as was his refusal to accept potentially compromising gifts from those he ordained. He gave 'the price of at least fifteen men,' a huge sum, to the brehons, and 'paid kings' sons to walk with me,' to try and make his journeys safer.

ACCUSATIONS
old sins and unorthodoxies

Patrick worked in Ireland for many years, but specific complaints against him surfaced in Britain. It seems he was accused of using his mission for personal gain, spreading blasphemies and consorting with barbarian pagans, to which his reply was 'I am the letter of Christ,' thus applying St Paul's words to himself. God needed him to preach to this furthest corner of the earth so as to prepare the way for Christ's Second Coming.

Patrick's strong belief in his personal relationship with God was dangerously close to the teaching of Pelagius, which were declared heretical because he said believers could find personal paths to God. This denied the Church's monopoly on access to God, an essential tool of the Roman state religion, which preferred St Augustine's position that humans were so mired in sin that they were never free, and could only bridge the gulf between themselves and God through the Church. Indeed as Germanus of Auxerre and Palladius worked hard to eradicate 'Pelagianism' in Britain in the 420s, the Pope may have sent Palladius as 'first bishop to the Irish believers in Christ' to eliminate it there.

Patrick's British 'seniors' examined his case. An old friend then revealed 'things' Patrick had confessed, thirty years earlier, doing 'on one day, or rather in an hour, when I had no strength yet. God knows if I was even fifteen, and I did not yet believe in the living God'. These unnamed 'things' may well have been a youthful participation in Romano-British pagan cult rituals, which again could justify excommunication and removal from office.

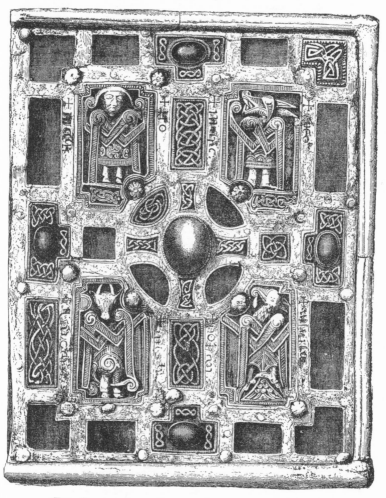

THE CUMDACH, OR CASE OF ST. MOLAISE'S GOSPELS.

LIGHT OF THE WORLD
a pagan heart?

I suspect Patrick was accused of pagan practices, as somebody seems to have related how he had cried out to the sun during his sleep paralysis. The Confession discusses this at length, but the surviving copies of the text say that he had called out 'Helias,' which must be a spelling alteration to make Helios look more like Elias, the Latin for Elijah, for Patrick admits crying out to the sun for help, but then excuses himself by saying that he had reacted in ignorance and concluding in very Christian terms: 'the sun will never reign, nor will its splendour last. All who worship it will find the punishment of misery, but we who believe and adore the true sun, Christ, will never die.'

'I was asleep, and Satan attacked me violently, something I shall remember as long as I am in this body. A huge rock fell on me, as it were, and I could not move my limbs. But whence did it come to my ignorant mind to call on Helias? At this I saw the sun rise in the sky and shouted Helias Helias with all my strength, and lo, the sun's splendour fell on me and at once scattered all this weight.'

Nevertheless Patrick was a most sincere Christian, albeit of the older, more Gnostic belief tradition taught by Pelagius, and which was seemingly widespread amongst the Romano-British, that believers were free and could develop their own relationship with the divine.

4ᵗʰ century mosaic from Rudston, N. Yorkshire

19

INTO THE DARK AGES
with the vestiges of empire

One Romano–British group used extreme violence against Patrick's mission, doubtless justifying this slaughter of other Christians by the Augustinian idea of the 'just war'. He had given the sacraments to a large Irish group, presumably a tribal gathering, when they were attacked by the 'soldiers of Coroticus,' Ceredig in Welsh, a name which appears in British king lists as that of two sub-Roman rulers, in Strathclyde and north Wales. The soldiers then 'distributed baptised young women as prizes,' sold other captives to pagan Scoti and Picts, and 'replenished their homes with spoil from dead Christians.'

Patrick sent priests to demand the baptised women's release but the soldiers only laughed, so Patrick excommunicated them in his Letter as 'not citizens of the Holy Romans but of demons.' As for the tyrant Coroticus 'the riches he has unjustly collected will burst out of his stomach, the angel of death drags him, he will be ripped apart by raging dragons, a serpent's tongue shall kill him, and unquenchable fire engulf him.'

The Scoti are once again central to our story. These events must have happened in Ulster for Irish Scoti and Scottish Picts to feature, which makes a Strathclyde involvement feasible. Ironically the Romano-British world was dying; its organisation and industry had disintegrated, towns were half derelict, villas had become ruins or rough farmyards and British 'tyrants' ruled from strengthened hill forts, until an Anglo-Saxon revolt broke their rule in eastern Britain later in the century. Patrick however talks of Roman culture and order as normal, not realising, perhaps, the irreversibility of its decline.

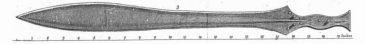

20

21

Tírechán & Muirchú's Patrick
making a saint

Copies of the Letter and Confession were probably preserved at Mochta's Louth monastery, and in the seventh century Patrick became revered. A hymn likened him to Peter and Paul, and Cummian told Iona's abbot that 'holy Patrick, our papa' brought their Easter computations. Then two clerics, Tírechán and Muirchú, wrote accounts of his life, saying he christianised virtually all Ireland himself and comparing him to Moses. Their Patrick constantly performs miracles, emphasising that he has access to powers far stronger than any pagan magic.

Tírechán concentrates on stories from Voclut and the West while Muirchú talks about the Northeast and Armagh, which claimed Patrick as its founder and was trying to establish its primacy in Ireland. He says Patrick first reached Ulster as bishop at Strangford Lough and 'hiding the boat went inland a little way to rest' where he met the swineherd of Dichu, who gave him his rath at Saul. Its barn became his church.

This tale even contains a fragment of Patrick's mother tongue. He swore Mudebroth at locals for digging a rath's ditch on a Sunday, which seems to be min Duw braut, 'by God's judgement' in Old Welsh. The phrase immediately won renown, as 'the next night a great wind arose, stirred up the sea and destroyed all the heathens' work.'

Tírechán says Patrick died at Saul, and adds that his angel ordered untamed oxen to be yoked to a cart bearing his body, and that they took it to Downpatrick. The sea raged until he was buried there, and flames shot out of his grave when it was disturbed.

St. Patrick met by Virgins in the Wood of Fochlut.

23

SLEMISH AND SKERRY
the pagan who would not yield

Tírechán and Muirchú both say that Patrick was slave to Miliucc, king or druid of the Braid Valley in north Antrim, and tended his herds near Slemish mountain. Muirchú says that when Patrick returned as bishop Miliucc would not submit, but brought his valuables into his house, and burnt them with him. Tírechán says Patrick taught Miliucc's children about Christ, with equally incendiary consequences. 'You poured fire into my son's mouth, which filled the lips of my daughters and they burnt to cinders' he protested, but Patrick retorted that the sparks of Christ's words made them 'vomit up their druid past.'

Tírechán says Patrick had his visions here, while his angel stood with one foot on Slemish and the other on Skerry hill a mile away. Supposedly Miliucc's house was here, and the angel's footprint is on a stone by Skerry church. A cross marked where Patrick stood below Slemish, a crag is Patrick's Seat, a stone is worn by his knees, the devil's footmark is on a rock in the river and below a cairn are the ashes of Miliucc's daughters.

In these accounts Patrick also cursed Miliucc's family to eternal subservience, which justified the Braid's conquest by the neighbouring kingdom of Dalriada. A church was later built on Skerry. The hill thus has curious echoes of Navan Fort, the sacred tribal hill of Ulster, where a large circular wood and thatch house was constructed, filled with stones, burnt and then buried so as to create a ritual centre in the Iron Age.

EASTER AT TARA
breaking the old order

Tírechán and Muirchú also both describe a decisive confrontation with pagan Ireland 'on the plain of Brega' where Patrick celebrated his first Easter as it was close to Tara, 'the centre of all paganism.' This was the great royal assembly hill of Meath, the central 'fifth' of Ireland, sacred to the goddess Medb Lethderg, with whom new kings mated. A late account of a different inauguration says that king mated with a white mare, before it was slaughtered, boiled and eaten; probably some similar rite happened at Tara.

A pagan festival was also happening that Easter. King Loiguire, a son of Niall of the Nine Hostages, had to light the new Spring fire, but Patrick lit his Easter fire first, so Loiguire brought his warriors and druids on twenty-seven chariots down to confront him, though one of them did honour him, 'Erc mac Dago, whose relics are now venerated in Slane.'

Muirchú says that one of the druids then derided Christianity so Patrick prayed, the druid was lifted up and dropped, smashing his skull on a rock. Tírechán says the druid went up 'almost to the sky' and came down 'frozen solid with hail and snow mixed with sparks of fire' and that the stone containing the frozen druid lies there still. Loiguire's forces then charged, but God brought down darkness and an earthquake, destroying them.

26

Left: Patrick arriving at Tara.
Above: Standing Stone at Tara.
Below: Tara medieval parish church

THE END OF PAGAN IRELAND
greater than the druids

Muirchú has Patrick enter Tara's feasting hall on Easter Monday, miraculously passing through closed doors. A druid offered him a drink, but let a drop fall from his cup into Patrick's, who prayed so his drink froze, and turning it upside down 'out fell the drop the druid had put in.'

More tests followed. A druid made snow fall on the plain, but could not remove it, so Patrick prayed and it vanished. The druid brought down fog, which he also could not disperse, but Patrick did, so fire tests took place. Tírechán and Muirchú describe different scenarios. In one a druid wore Patrick's chasuble and put his cloak on Patrick's boy assistant, in the other the druid stood in part of a house made with wet wood while the boy had the dry wood side. In both cases they were then torched, the druid burnt and the boy was unscathed, as was Patrick's chasuble.

Muirchú says King Loiguire then 'turned to the Eternal Lord God,' but Tírechán has him remain an unrepentant pagan, though one of his brothers believed, and was the founder of the Christian Uí Néill line. He gave Patrick land nearby, upon which he built his greatest church, Donaghpatrick, some sixty foot long. Patrick also gave communion at Cruachan, Connacht's assembly hill, to two of Loiguire's daughters, who wanted to see Christ's face and immediately died. He built a church on their ferta, a pagan burial mound.

ARMAGH
building an Irish Rome

Armagh was named after the mythological Macha, who gave birth to twins after being forced to race against horses and cursed the Ulstermen to labour pains in times of need. It is in sight of her other hill, Emain Macha, Navan, Ulster's legendary royal capital.

In Muirchú's first tale Patrick cursed the horse of Armagh's owner, Daire, for grazing on land he had given. It died, and Daire fell ill when he told his men to kill Patrick, who had holy water sprinkled on man and horse, reviving them.

The second, like the Saul story, contains a garbled phrase, Grazacham, the Latin *gratias agam*, 'Let me give thanks.' Daire had a 'marvellous cauldron from overseas which held triple measure.' He gave it to Patrick, who replied 'Grazacham'.

Daire remarked 'this man is a fool only to say Grazacham for so wonderful a cauldron,' and told his slaves to get it back. Patrick only said 'Grazacham, take it' and Daire responded 'Grazacham for the giving, Grazacham for the taking. These Grazachams mean so much I must return it,' adding 'you are obstinate and imperturbable. I give you the land you asked for.'

In the third Patrick and Daire find a doe and fawn lying on the hill where a church altar was to be built. Their companions made to kill them, but Patrick took them to a slope and let them go. Muirchú adds 'there are traces of the miracle to the present day.'

Above: The town of Armagh.
Below: Pillar stone at Kilnasaggart near Armagh. Its ca. 700 inscription says the place had been put "under the protection of Peter the Apostle," probably by Armagh.

VOCLUT

near the western shore

Tírechán relates how Patrick founded a church near Voclut wood and then ordained Mucneus as its bishop, 'for God told him to leave aside the law and consecrate bishops and deacons in that country.' Two bishops were required to perform consecrations, so Patrick was breaking Church rules. He also gave Mucneus the 'seven books of the law' and 'blessed a place by Voclut wood' for two girls who took the veil.

While in the West he baptised a baby in its dying mother's womb, built a church from sods in a place with no stone or timber and consecrated others. Near Castlebar there was a square pagan well called Slán, health. Gold and silver offerings were left in it, and water oozed out round a rectangular stone, behind which were supposed to lie a seer's bones. Patrick had the stone pulled out, and made the well Christian. The stone still lay there in Tírechán's day.

There is also a wonder tale about a Neolithic chambered tomb. At Dichuil Patrick was shown a grave of marvellous size, 120 feet long. He struck it, and a giant rose up. 'I wish you well, holy man, for raising me,' he said, so Patrick baptised him, and he fell back.

WONDER TALES
and curses

Muirchú and Tírechán's Patrick was effectively performing spells like a powerful wizard – a talent common to many popular saints in the early Christian world.

When Patrick once saw two brothers with raised swords, preparing to fight each other, he froze them. Their row was over the ownership of some land, so he made them give it for a church, where rests 'the craftsman Cuanu, brother of Sachellus, bishop of Baslick.'

He cursed the river Duff to be always empty of fish as the locals would give him none, and another when two disciples drowned. A ford rose up in the Bush so he could cross over to Dunseverick, to consecrate Olcán and give him relics of Peter and Paul. He remained dry in a rainstorm, cursed the field of an opponent and made a druid die and burn from the opposite bank of the river Moy.

Once Patrick asked a dead man about the cross over his grave. He replied he was pagan and the cross was there by mistake, so Patrick set it over the right grave. Wicked Coroticus he turned into a fox, and one night the charioteer lost their horses in the dark. Patrick raised his hand, his fingers shone like lanterns and the horses were found.

CROAGH PATRICK
a sacred mountain

Croagh Patrick or the Reek, overlooking Clew Bay in Mayo, is the greatest pilgrimage centre associated with Patrick, and possibly also the source of prehistoric Irish gold.

Tirechán's Patrick came with hundreds of followers, built a cairn over his charioteer's grave, after a pagan had killed him, and spent forty days on the Reek, like Moses or Christ, while 'mighty birds flew round him so he could see neither sky, sea nor land.'

By the eighth century hymn the birds were angelic. They sang and beat a lake with their wings so it sparkled like silver. A century later they were demonic. Patrick rang Saint Brigid's bell at them, threw it and a piece broke off. Until the last of the Geraghty family emigrated about 1840 they were guardians of this battered bell, the Clog Dubh. Pilgrims had to kiss it and pass it three times round their bodies before climbing the Reek.

Patrick also defeated the devil's mother here, the serpent Corra, and women wanting babies spent the night on a boulder, his bed. The pilgrimage is on Domhnach Chrom Dubh, the last Sunday of July. Crom Dubh is a god usually disguised as a pagan lord, and the date concerns the pagan feast of Lughnasa, the old harvest festival.

LUGHNASA HILLS & WATERS
sheltering old beliefs

Many Lughnasa assemblies were on sacred hills, so Patrick set seven guardians, like Enoch's seven angels, in its mountains: the Reek, Benbulben, Slieve Beagh, Slieve Gua, Clonard mountain and Slieve Donard.

Inside Slieve Donard, nearly three thousand feet high, lives Donard, a pagan king's son, in chambers under the megalithic tomb on its peak, to 'raise Patrick's relics just before Doomsday.' Patrick had tamed this king's bull, then slaughtered it, to his fury, so he tied the bones in its hide and revived it, fiercer than ever. Until the Famine pilgrims gathered at the tomb, by then renamed Donard's Chapel, to hear mass at the end of July.

At Cashel, Munster's sacred hill, Patrick met the poet giant Oisín, who fought a raging bull and thrashed vast quantities of corn. At Teltown in Meath, Patrick condemned King Loiguire to the Black Lake, the short road to hell, in which lurked a serpent. In 1168 the last High King, Rory O'Connor, was proclaimed there, mock battles took place in nearby lakes, and couples married or divorced each other by declaration, in 'Teltown Marriages.'

At Carmain, the Leinster assembly site, St Patrick blessed the well, at Mám Éan he banished another fierce bull to a lake, and in Sligo faced the Corra again, who had polluted all Irish waters so Patrick struck Tullaghan rock, sweet water burst forth, he drank until his strength revived, and banished her for ever.

St. Patrick Taming the Mad Ox.

AWAY WITH THE FAIRIES

storms about heaven

Patrick also converted Crom Dubh, who became so poor that he had to collect firewood from the forest. The Hosts of the Air, the fairies, then pulled it off his back and made him promise to ask Patrick after Sunday mass if they could go to heaven too. They had always been friends of men, protecting their households and doing many chores, and would gather Crom Dubh's firewood for ever if he would do them this favour.

Patrick's response was that 'priests' lovers, unbaptised infants and Airy Demons' were excluded from heaven 'until the Last Judgement at the very least.' He told Crom Dubh to go into the wood, dig a grave, lie in it, and then make a cross over himself with his tools. He was then to tell the fairies of their fate. When he did they screamed and stormed, and tore the woods apart with tempests, but Crom Dubh came to no harm. When all was quiet again he went home safely.

Ever since then storms occur wherever the fairies go, and they do what mischief they can. Since then too the Sunday on which Patrick answered their question, Domhnach Chrom Dubh, has constant bad weather even though it is in harvest-time.

HOLY ANCESTORS
awkward relations

Early genealogists had to show that their lords were of the very best stock, and proper biblical origins were given to family trees. All good Irishmen come from Milesius, descendant of Scota, the pharaoh's daughter who found Moses in the bullrushes, and her line goes back to Noah's son Japhet, but getting close to Patrick was also essential. Fortunately he had many potential ancestors in his household, including charioteers, blacksmiths, brewers and embroiderers, but better still there were his sisters.

The most adventurous of these was Lupita. She was forever getting into awkward situations. Once Patrick found her at midnight in her nephew St Mel's bed, but she explained that he always went to confession then, so she would sneak into his bed to wrap herself in his bedclothes and be impregnated by his sanctity.

Mel then proved that he still was in God's good favours by ploughing a field, whereupon salmon jumped miraculously out of the furrows, but when St MacNissi of Conor interfered with Lupita, Patrick made his lecherous hand drop off, and when Patrick found her in flagrante with Colman of Clann Bressail he leapt into his chariot, drove over her three times in honour of the Trinity, and said a mass to get her into heaven.

One of her many children then begged Patrick to see to it that they could go to heaven too, which he arranged. At least it gave the genealogists something for their family trees.

St. Patrick showing the People the Book of the Four Gospels.

GLASTONBURY
an English home?

In the English West Country, where Patrick's life may well have begun, several tales connect him with Glastonbury abbey. It was home to a plethora of cults, and was the goal of many pilgrims in the Middle Ages. Arthur's tomb is here, and Joseph of Arimathea stuck his staff into the ground near the abbey, during his visit, where it grew into the Glastonbury Thorn. Patrick, they said, spent his last thirty years here and was one of its founders, along with Joseph, Jesus, and saints Phagan, Deruvian and Glasteing of the eight-footed pig.

Glastonbury claimed several impressive connections with Ireland, though sadly these seem to be mainly the product of some profitable monastic wishful thinking. Saint Bridget lived nearby for a long time, they said, and three highly suspect tenth century copies of early Anglo-Saxon charters dedicate the church to Patrick as well as Mary. Indeed Patrick's tomb was close to the high altar. It was explained that there had been two Patricks in Ireland, and that Glastonbury was the final home of the senior one, Palladius, whose mission, they said, had failed.

'Patrick was the first teacher of the Irish, they say, but as he could not correct them he left on pilgrimage. He came to Glastonbury monastery and here finished his life, famous for his miraculous powers. So it is that his bones are here.'

Left: entrance to Glastonbury's Mary chapel, site of the first church in Britain. Above: The Holy Thorn, brought by Joseph of Arimathea. Below: Bligh Bond's fanciful drawing of the first church at Glastonbury in 37 AD.

GLASTON: THE FIRST CHRISTIAN SETTLEMENT: A·D·37. WITH WATTLE CHURCH.
COPYRIGHT 1939.

RELICS
sacred remains

Inevitably Patrick relics were cherished. His 'insignia' still existed circa 640, Tírechán knew of a tooth and a vestment, his satchel was in Meath, a bishop had his tiny shrine hanging round his neck and his cloth was stolen by the Vikings. Tírechán talks of the many ecclesiastical objects Patrick brought, and of fifty bells that he took across the Shannon. One of these got a lavish shrine from a high king and the abbot of Armagh, another has PATRICI engraved on it, the bell from the Reek is appropriately battered, and a contender for the MacDonnell chieftaincy was cursed with one in 1602, but none is in fact earlier than the ninth century.

The Normans eagerly identified Patrick's tomb at Downpatrick, captured his crosier, formerly Jesus's staff, which God gave Patrick as he set out for Ireland, and kept it in Dublin with his portable altar, where it was burnt by Tudor reformers. A king of Connacht gave the tooth a shrine which a Norman embellished, another was made for a hand and an Earl of Ormond ordered one for a piece of Patrick's skull.

This relic cult continued more modestly under English Protestant rule. In the late 1600s a silver container was made for Patrick's jaw, and another was commissioned for his thumb in 1737 by a Catholic archbishop of Armagh, who gave it to nuns in Drogheda.

47

LOUGH DERG
purging sins

Droves of medieval pilgrims visited Patrick's Purgatory on Saint's Island in Lough Derg, but its priory was profiting so outrageously from them that a pope closed it in the 1490s. The pilgrims thereafter went to Station Island and in 1632 a Protestant bishop, James Spottiswoode, destroyed the Purgatory, 'a poor beggarly hole, made with some stones lay'd together with men's hands without any great art and after covered with earth.'

Patrick atoned for his sins here, and the pilgrims went through great rigours. After fifteen days fasting they were shut for a whole day in its dark interior, a stone passageway leading to a chamber, like a megalithic tomb, and the subject of a medieval best seller. A twelfth century crusader, Knight Owen, saw robed figures in it who admonished him before demons led him to where souls were pierced by hot nails, boiled, frozen, squashed by vast toads and nailed to burning wheels. They went to a crag where icy winds blew souls into foul waters, to be trampled on by devils, and saw the damned in the Pit of Hell. Owen slithered over the Bridge of Impossibilities to see a gate to heaven, and viewed Paradise from a mountain peak.

Others had similar experiences and one said 'a certain hot vapour rose' from a covered cleft leading down to Hell, after which they had 'marvellous dreams.' Over 350 medieval copies still exist of Knight Owen's tale, which must have inspired Dante.

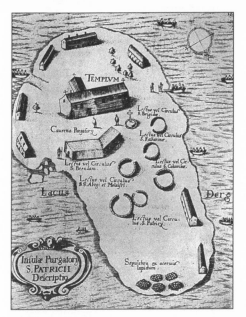

SNAKES AND SHAMROCKS
green salad and serpents

We are told there are no snakes in Ireland because Patrick banished them, a tale first recorded by the Norman Giraldus Cambrensis in his history of Ireland.

'Of all kinds of reptiles only those that are not harmful are found in Ireland. It has no poisonous reptiles, serpents, toads, frogs, tortoises or scorpions, and no dragons, though it has spiders, leeches and lizards, but these are all harmless. Some indulge in the pleasant conjecture that Saint Patrick and other saints purged the island of harmful animals, but it is more probable that from the earliest times, and long before the founding of the Faith, the island was naturally without these things.'

But there were many terrifying serpents. One at Teltown ate cattle, another lived in Lough Derg, Corra was the devil's mother, and a druid became one to avoid Patrick, who condemned him to stay like that until Judgement Day, brooding deep in Manann pond.

Tradition says Patrick explained the Trinity to the Irish with a shamrock, the trefoil wood sorrel, which grew wild and nourished the needy. In earlier times the Irish ate them fresh or baked with meal and butter into shamrock bread. Patrick is first depicted holding one on coins of the 1640s and by 1680 the Irish did 'superstitiously wear shamrogues' on his day. Finally, in 1727 it was recorded for the first time 'that by this three-leaved grass he emblematically set forth the mystery of the Holy Trinity.'

St Patrick's Day
new world fun and old world rites

Nowadays we think of enormous parades on the seventeenth of March where all and sundry proclaim Irish roots. Appropriately, the first one was in Boston in 1737. Everywhere now beer turns green, as do teeth, bagpipes and hair, but wood sorrel is no longer shamrock. That honour has been transferred to an inedible clover which only reached Ireland four hundred years ago.

In the Irish countryside things were a little different. Spring festival customs attached themselves to Patrick much like Lughnasa, so St Patrick's was the day for planting lilies and the first potatoes. On the summit of St Patrick's Hill near Straffan, another tribal assembly site, a mass was said. Afterwards the boys threw lumps of earth at each other, for this was the day to first turn the ground. Below the hill are a well and a tiny church they say he built, a place of new beginnings: elsewhere farmers started working the ground with the spade again on the Seventeenth, or the plough cut its first furrow.

Water in streams and wells lose their winter cold then, for Patrick warms the stones, and he has wells all over Ireland. Also, every green rush grows with a brown tip because he cursed them for pricking him when he once sat down on them.

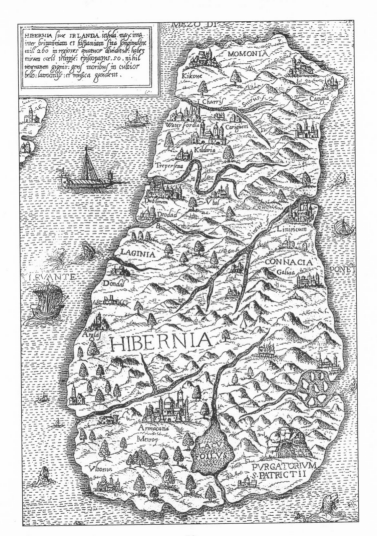

HIBERNIA sive IRLANDA. insula maxima
inter britanniam et hispaniam sita longitudine
mill 260 in regiones quatuor dividitur: habet
minam coeli temperie: episcopatus. 50. nihil
venenatum gignit: gens moribus in cultior
bello: lavoaniis: et musica gaudent.

MEZO DI

MOMONIA

Kikone

Charri   Suirius   Cacigia

Waurfordia   Carigium

Kildaria

Treperseua

Dublinum   Vtal

Drodad

Liminicum

LAGINIA   CONNACIA   PONET

Galua

LEVANTE

Dondal

Ardal

HIBERNIA

Armacana
Metrop

Vltonia

LACV
FOILVS

PVRGATORIVM
S. PATRICTII

SAINT PADDY
a fine figure of a saint

The stereotype Patrick, the national patron saint, is not a figure he would recognise, though he might enjoy having the shamrock as his legacy. He devoted his life to bringing Christian concepts to country people, and it certainly is a metaphor to be proud of. Moreover Patrick still has much to say. His belief in direct personal relationships with God and inner spiritual experiences should appeal to many who are searching for a path.

Irishmen are anyway generally pleased to be called Paddies. They are proud of their patron saint, and his robust personality. He has even inspired a gently witty Music Hall song.

Oh Saint Patrick was a gentleman
Who came of decent people
He built a church in Dublin town
And put on it a steeple.

Oh the Wicklow hills are very high
And so's the Hill of Howth sir,
But there's a hill much bigger still
Much bigger than them both sir.

'Twas on the top of that high hill
That Patrick preached his sarmint
And drove the frogs into the bogs
And banished all the varmint

SITES ASSOCIATED WITH ST PATRICK

Armagh, originally *Ard Macha*, an ancient hill site dedicated to *Macha*, a pagan cult figure whose name also occurs nearby at Navan, *Emhain Macha*, the legendary royal capital of Ulster. Tírechán gives three traditions about Patrick founding his church here. Armagh claimed Patrick made it his Episcopal seat, and thus it was by rights Ireland's religious capital, as they also claimed that Patrick alone had made Ireland Christian.

Bannavem Taberniae/Bannaveta Berniae, the Romano-British village near which was Patrick's family's *vilulla*, a small villa. Its location is unknown.

Baslick, co. Roscommon, Tírechán says Patrick buried 'the craftsman Cuanu, brother of Sachellus, bishop of Basilice Móire,' the Big Basilica. Sachellus is possibly pre-Patrician, Baslick is on a hilltop close to the important tribal assembly hill of Cruachan (q.v.).

Benbulben, co. Sligo, a table top mountain, one of the seven inside which Patrick set guardians to watch over Ireland until the Second Coming. There are no other Christian traditions about Benbulben, but several in the Fenian legends.

Braid Valley, co. Antrim, the kingdom of the Braid Valley identified by Tírechán and Muirchú (ca. 670) as the place where Patrick was a slave, and that the local king or druid, Miliucc, was his slave master. The Braid, which was probably still pagan, was annexed by Dalriada, the neighbouring kingdom, by the seventh century, and the Patrick stories may have helped justify this. He cursed Miliucc's family as ever unfit to rule.

Bush river, co. Antrim, in Muirchú's account Patrick had to cross this river to get to Dunseverick (q.v.) to consecrate Olcán; a ford miraculously rose up to let him cross it. Carmain, the Leinster tribal assembly hill, site unknown, Patrick blessed a well here. Named after a mythological female called Carman.

Cashel, co. Tipperary, Munster's royal hill. In the *Tripartite Life* Patrick met Oisín here, a mythological figure and the legendary father of poetry in Ireland.

Conor, co. Antrim, ancient capital seat of a local kingdom; according to the *Tripartite Life* St MacNissi of Conor interfered with Patrick's wayward sister Lupita so Patrick made his lecherous hand drop off.

Clonard, one of the seven mountains inside which Patrick set guardians to watch over Ireland until the Second Coming. A monastery founded here by St Finian circa 520

Croagh Patrick, co. Mayo, the greatest pilgrimage centre for Patrick. It may have been originally venerated as a source of prehistoric gold. Tírechán's Patrick spent forty days on its peak, while 'mighty birds flew round him so he could see neither sky sea nor land.'

Cruachan, Connacht's royal tribal assembly hill; Tírechán says that Patrick gave the sacraments here to two of Loiguire's daughters, who then died, and that he built a church on top of their *ferta*, or pagan burial mound, thus Christianising a pagan site.

Donaghpatrick, co. Meath, according to Tírechán Loiguire's brother gave this site near Tara to Patrick, who built his great church here, sixty foot long.

Downpatrick, co. Down, Tírechán says untamed oxen brought a cart with Patrick's body from Saul (q.v.) to Downpatrick, so he was then buried here. A stone beside the cathedral marks the reputed site of Patrick's grave

Duff river, cos. Sligo & Donegal, in the *Tripartite Life* was cursed by Patrick to be empty of fish after local fishermen refused him any; he reversed the curse when some boys gave him a fish. Two holy wells nearby are visited on St Patrick's day: St Patrick's Well and the Shaving Well where Patrick and his followers shaved off their beards.

Dunseverick, co. Antrim, a capital seat of the kingdom of Dalriada; Muirchú says Patrick consecrated Olcán here and gave him relics of Peter and Paul, one of a few accounts of European relics in Ireland in the earliest Christian period.

Dunshaughlin, co. Meath the possibly pre-Patrician church site on a hill near Tara (q.v.) of St Secundinus. It suggests an early Christian presence here.

Foghill, co. Sligo, probably the Voclut of the *Confession*. St Patrick's holy well is the only remnant of ancient veneration.

Glastonbury Abbey, Somerset, claimed, from the 10th century onwards, that St Patrick's grave was here. The stories are actually about Palladius, the bishop sent to Ireland in 431, the senior St Patrick of some traditions. 'Patrick was the first teacher of the Irish, they say, but as he could not correct them he left on pilgrimage. He came to Glastonbury monastery and here finished his life, famous for his miraculous powers.'

Lough Derg, co. Donegal, from the medieval period onwards Patrick's Purgatory on Saint's Island was an important place of pilgrimage, as it was believed that he had fasted and prayed here as a penance for his own sins.

Louth, co. Louth, reputedly the first Irish monastery, founded by Mochta, a Romano-British follower of Patrick; probably Patrick's Confession and Letter were preserved here before they were copied into the Book of Armagh circa 810.

Manann pond, co. Monaghan, a druid turned himself into a serpent in this lake to avoid Patrick, who then condemned him to stay there until Judgement Day.

Moy river, co. Mayo, Muirchú has Patrick curse a druid whom he sees on the Moy's opposite bank, with the result that he died on the spot and burst into flames. Near the river at Ballina is a well where the *Tripartite Life* says Patrick baptised a local prince, Eochaid, and preached to the people of the region.

Saul, co. Down, according to Muirchú when Patrick first landed as a bishop on the shore near here a local, Dichu, gave him his rath on this hill, and Patrick used its barn, Irish *sabhail*, as his church. Two miles away at Raholp is a 10th century church and holy well, there are also the Struell Wells, associated with Patrick and much visited by pilgrims.

Skerry Hill, co. Antrim, traditionally the site of Miliucc's house, in which he burnt himself rather than submit to Patrick, who then built a church on it (see Braid Valley).

Slán, Ballintober co. Mayo, Tírechán says there was a square well here called Slán, health, a place of pagan worship. The pagans left gold and silver offerings in it, and its waters oozed out round a rectangular stone reputedly covering a wizard's bones. Patrick pulled out the stone, blessed the well, baptised his disciple Cainneach in its water and built a church beside it for him. The stone was there in Tírechán's day.

Slieve Beagh, co. Meath, one of the seven mountains inside which Patrick's guardians keep watch. There are fifteen prehistoric barrow graves on its summit.

Slieve Donard, co. Down, one of the seven mountains inside which Patrick set guardians to watch over Ireland. Donard, son of the last pagan king lives in chambers under the megalithic tomb on its peak beside which a yearly mass was said until the 1840s.

Slieve Gua, co. Waterford, one of the seven mountains inside which Patrick set guardians to watch over Ireland until the Second Coming; it is now the Knockmealdown mountains and is in an early triad along with the Wicklow Hills and Slemish (q.v.).

Slemish, co. Antrim, in Tírechán and Muirchú's accounts it was not 'near the wood of Voclut' (q.v.), but on the slopes of this mountain that young Patrick as a slave tended the herds of his master Miliucc (*see Braid Valley*).

Slane, co. Meath, the hill near Tara upon which Tírechán and Muirchú say that Patrick lit the first Pascal fire in Ireland, leading to the great confrontation with Loiguire, the pagan High King of Ireland. One of Loiguire's men, Erc mac Dago, went over to Patrick, and that 'his relics are now venerated in Slane.' A ruined monastery is on its summit.

Straffan, co. Kildare, St Patrick's Hill, a tribal assembly site. Mass was said here on St Patrick's Day; afterwards boys threw lumps of earth and visits were made to Patrick's chapel and holy well below the hill.

Tara, co. Meath, the great royal assembly hill of the central 'fifth' of Ireland, sacred to the goddess Medb Lethderg; Tírechán and Muirchú say that Patrick had his decisive confrontation with the High King 'on the plain of Brega' below Tara after lighting his first Pascal fire (see Slane). Patrick miraculously enters Tara's feasting hall the next day through closed doors, and wins a series of magical contests with Loiguire's druids.

Teltown, co. Meath, an assembly hill near Tara named after the god Lugh's stepmother Tailtiu and christianised by Patrick. In 1168 the last High King, Rory O'Connor, was proclaimed here, mock battles took place in nearby lakes, and until the nineteenth century couples would marry or divorce each other by declaration, in 'Teltown Marriages.'

Tullaghan rock, Sligo, during his struggle with the Corra Patrick, like Moses, struck this rock with a stick, after she poisoned all wells. Sweet water burst forth, and the well was a Wonder of Ireland in the Middle Ages, as its waters ebbed and flowed with the sea.

Voclut (*see Foghill*), Patrick says in his *Confession* that he lived as a slave 'near the wood of Voclut'. Tírechán says Patrick founded a church here, ordained Mucneus as its bishop and 'blessed a place by Voclut wood' for two women who took the veil.

CHRONOLOGY

NB: The Irish annals' dates given are all open to debate.

312 – 37 Constantine gives Christianity official status in the Roman Empire.

361 – 3 Emperor Julian attempts to restore pagan worship (this policy reversed after 363).

367 Picts and Scots conspire with local troops to pillage large parts of Roman Britain.

381 Statue of Goddess Victory removed from Roman senate.

395 Pagan worship made a criminal offence in the Roman Empire.

396 St Victiricius or Victoricius of Rouen in Britain, to settle issues concerning the local bishops; probably a Romano-Briton, he had initiated missionary activities amongst the barbarians in Flanders. Victoricius is the only name mentioned in Patrick's *Confession*.

397 death of St Martin of Tours, who brought Christianity to the rural poor and introduced monasticism to western Gaul.

398 St Augustine's Confession.

ca. 405-20 vicious dispute between the British or Irish theologian Pelagius (he is described as a 'Scotus' who lived on porridge by St Jerome) and Augustine about God's relationship to man. Pelagius said that believers can find paths to God without needing the intermediary of the church, Augustine that human sinfulness makes this impossible.

410 Alaric the Goth sacks Rome.

post 410 Britain, becomes isolated from the Roman Empire, and has to look to its own organisation & defence.

415-18 Pelagianism attacked by papacy and then declared a heresy.

427-9 Palladius negotiates between the Pope and bishop Germanus of Auxerre about the suppression of Pelagian teachings in Britain.

429 Germanus in Britain suppressing Pelagianism.

431 Palladius, now Pope Celestine's secretary, sent as bishop to Christians in Ireland.

432 earliest date in various Irish annals for Patrick's arrival in Ireland as bishop: "Bishop Patrick begins to baptise the Scoti." (*Annals of Inisfallen*)

433 "Conversion of the Scoti" (*Annals of Inisfallen*)

443 "Patrick the bishop was flourishing in our province." (*Annals of Ulster*)

444 "Armagh was founded by Patrick, 1,194 years after Rome". (*Annals of Ulster*)

457 "The repose of Old Patrick" [Palladius] (*Annals of Ulster & Annals of Four Masters*)

Armagh founded, and Patrick has an "archbishop's city" built there as "head of the churches in Ireland." (*Annals of the Four Masters*)

458 "The repose of Old Patrick" [Palladius] (*Annals of Boyle*)

461 "Here some place the death of Patrick" [Palladius] (*Annals of Ulster*)

489 "The repose of St Cianán, to whom Patrick gave a gospel" (*Annals of Ulster*)

492 "The Irish say that Patrick the archbishop died ... Patrick preached in Ireland for eighty years, and God restored to life forty people for him. He founded 365 churches, made as many bishops and baptised 1,200." (*Annals of Ulster*)

496 "The repose of Patrick on the 17th March" (*Annals of Inisfallen*)

circa 670-90 Tírechán and Muirchú, two Irish clerics, compile information about Patrick, Tírechán primarily in south-east Ulster, Muirchú in Connacht

Patrick's angel standing on Slemish and Skerry